LOVE IS LOVE

REAL TRUE LOVE
IS
COLORBLIND

Audrey Cunningham

Love is Love: Real True Love is Colorblind

ISBN 979-8-9886760-2-7

Published by

Emerge Publishing Group LLC

Riviera Beach, Fl 33404

Love is Love: Real

True Love is Colorblind

Printed in the United States of America

DEDICATION

This book is dedicated to our beloved family:

Walter's Parents

Lester and Allean Cunningham,

Audrey's Parents

William and Elizabeth Bryant

Our Children

Walter Jr., Cory and Shayna Cunningham

TABLE OF CONTENTS

Part III
Testimonials of Love

INTRODUCTION

This is not your typical love story about an interracial couple; one black, the other white, who had fallen in love with one another. The title of this book is Love is Love: Real: True Love is Colorblind.

This title is about relationships with people. We all are God-created individuals and human beings. Love is the complete component and the key.

Love is an action word. It goes beyond a word, feelings, red heart-shaped images and emojis. People can say the words "I Love You" every day and really have no concept or know the true meaning of what real true love is. They are saying it because it just sounds good to say.

As I previously mentioned, love is an action word. You must do something to show to the other person that you love and care about them and their well-being. Love is the greatest commandment there is. The definitions of colorblind are: 1. Unable to distinguish certain colors, or (rarely in humans) any colors at all. 2. Not influenced by racial prejudice.

This world would truly be a better place to live in if some people in our society were truly colorblind and see other people darker than themselves as human beings regardless of their skin tone or complexions. They should always be treated with respect no matter what their ethnicity or race is, whether they are Black, White, Hispanic, Asian, Indian or mixed races.

This is a real true-life story of two grown men, one white, one black whose lives crossed paths under unpleasant circumstances. Over time this evolved into a loving relationship. I hope that this book will truly touch your heart and human spirit.

PART I

LOVE IS COLORBLIND

Chapter 1

MR. CHARLIE

They first encountered one another in 1990. The first man's name was Charlie Waychoff. He was an older white man and a Veteran of the 1953 Korean War. The other man's name is Walter Cunningham Sr. who is a black man. Walter Cunningham Sr. is my husband. He was about thirty when he first met Charlie.

If you were to ever meet Walter, you definitely wouldn't forget him. He loves to spread love wherever he goes. He is very kind, considerate, selfless, courteous and the most personable human being you will ever meet. He is the same every day of his life. He is never moody and is always warm and friendly. He is no joke! He keeps it real! He will talk real straight talk to you about whatever the subject is and will not sugar coat anything.

During this time, in our family's history, Mr. Charlie Waychoff was our neighbor who lived a few doors down from us. Mr. Waychoff was not a friendly man. He was a mean person, especially to people of color. My husband and I found out exactly what type of individual he was when our two small sons came home from a day of playing near Charlie's house. They told us what he said to them.

Kids will be kids and while riding their bicycles they rode their bikes into Mr. Charlie's yard. He yelled and cursed at them and called them a name other than their real names. He said to them, "Get out of my yard Nigger."

As you can imagine, this did not sit well with us as parents, especially after hearing what was told to us by our children. The word "nigger" is very racist and offensive to people of color. It is totally unacceptable and should not be tolerated by anyone.

As black people, we did not create ourselves. God created us all—every race and ethnicity. We were created in His image and His likeness and He loves us all the same.

No one should ever be disrespected, belittled, insulted to feel less than just because of the color of their skin. My husband was very angry and upset about what occurred and did like any good father would have done. He went to pay Mr. Charlie a visit to let him know how he felt. He told him not to ever again call our children nigger or curse at them.

Walter held himself together and showed total restraint and control when he could have lost control and threw punches at Mr. Charlie. This was not a new experience for Walter, Sr. As a boy and young man growing up in Central Florida on occasions, he was also called out of his name and was called the "N" word by some white people.

So you can imagine how he felt having gone through this same thing when he was younger and unfortunately experiencing it again with his own children. He is a father who is a protector and a defender of our family. Children are innocent. They are not born with prejudice. When they are young, they play with each other and do not see color. Little white children will play with little black children and vice versa, little black children will play with little white children and they all get along with each other.

Unfortunately, children are taught to show prejudice by some racist white adults in their family. They are told that black people or a black person is bad. They believe the white race is superior and black people are inferior.

Chapter 2

"MY ENCOUNTER WITH MR. CHARLIE"

Below is what our oldest son, Walter Cunningham Jr. who is now forty-one years old said about his first experience meeting with Mr. Charlie.

"I remember being ten years old playing around on Silver Beach Road in Lake Park, Florida. Mr. Charlie lived a few houses down from where we lived.

I remember his circular driveway very clearly. My brother Cory and I would ride our bicycles around it and take off back home. It was like our route that we would take.

One particular afternoon, we were riding our bikes and we saw Mr. Charlie sitting near his truck in the circular drive. That didn't stop my brother and I from riding our bikes. We continued to ride around the driveway when suddenly, Mr. Charlie became very angry and started using the "N" word."

Our youngest son, Cory Cunningham who was seven years old at the time, now thirty-seven years old remembered about their encounter with Mr. Charlie.

He vividly recalled Mr. Charlie yelling at them saying, "Niggers don't be riding in my yard."

Chapter 3

ENEMIES CAN BE FRIENDS

My husband once told me, "You cannot beat hate out of a man; you have to love it out of him" and that is exactly what he did. He loved the hate out of Charlie and he became one of his best lifelong friends until the end. They were friends for over twenty-six years until Charlie passed away on December 31, 2017 in Climax, Michigan at the age of 84.

After the visitation with Walter, Charlie discontinued harassing our children and the neighborhood children playing outside near his home. Later on, Walter and Charlie began to talk to each other on a regular basis on friendlier terms.

Charlie was a military veteran who was disabled. He had serious health problems with both of his hips. The problems with his hips became so severe that at times, it was extremely painful and difficult for him to walk. When he did walk, he walked with a noticeable limp.

He was a widower; he had two young adult children. His children had their own share of problems and at times did not get along well with their father.

One day, Charlie confided in Walter and told him that he could barely walk and needed to go the Veteran's Administration Hospital located in Miami, Florida. He needed to see a doctor because his hip condition was steadily getting worse.

Walter told me that he was going to take off from work one day and drive Charlie to the VA hospital in Miami. I asked him why was he taking him to Miami to see a doctor. I reminded him that Charlie had two grown children and they should be helping their father go to the doctor. My husband disagreed with me and told me that was something that he had to do. I admit, I was angry and upset with him and told him he was crazy for taking off from work to take Charlie to the VA hospital.

Subsequently, he did what he said he was going to do. He took Charlie to the VA hospital. The doctor visit was not a good one. The doctor informed him of the deteriorating condition of his hip and recommended that he would eventually need to have hip replacement surgery.

When Charlie returned home from the doctor's visit a short time later, the pain became more unbearable. Charlie decided to have the hip replacement surgery on his right hip. During that time, Palm Beach County did not have a VA hospital so Charlie once again had to return to the VA hospital in Miami, Florida to have his hip surgery. Walter took off from work again and drove Charlie to the VA hospital to have his surgery.

He had to remain in the VA hospital a few days after the surgery. In addition, he also had to go through the rehabilitation process and learn how to walk again with his new right hip.

The day finally came when Charlie was released from the VA hospital. Once again, Walter volunteered to take off from his job and drove to Miami to pick up Charlie from the hospital and brought him back to his home in Lake Park, Florida.

After Charlie returned home, Walter went over to his house regularly to help him with whatever he needed help with. He cooked for him, cleaned his house, did his laundry, shopped at the grocery store for him, got his medications and helped bathe and bandage his wounds. He also assisted him with going to the bathroom. He continued to do this until he was strong enough and well enough to get back on his feet. Charlie's condition improved and got better after the surgery on his right hip. He no longer had any pain in his right hip area.

In 1994, I was very homesick and wanted to return back to my hometown of Ocala, Florida. I talked it over with my husband and he encouraged me to move back to Ocala with our three children. He stayed and worked in Palm Beach.

He remained in Lake Park and continued to work at Pratt & Whitney Aircraft. However, he commuted back and forth to Ocala over the weekends to be with us. During this time we were purchasing our first home which was a duplex. We lived on one side which was a two bedroom and one bathroom and rented the other side out which was also two bedrooms and one bathroom.

After a while, Walter decided instead of living in our side of the duplex, he decided to rent it out to earn extra money. The duplex has a great big back yard. He parked our family's van in the backyard and stayed in it. He also slept in it at night. Walter lived in the van for approximately one and a half years.

Chapter 4

A FRIEND IN NEED IS A FRIEND INDEED

Charlie later found out that Walter was living out of his van. He talked to him about it. He invited and insisted that Walter move in with him. He had an extra room in his apartment for him to stay in. Walter decided to take him up on his offer and moved in with him.

Shortly thereafter, Charlie's left hip started bothering him and giving him problems. It steadily became worse and worse. Eventually he had to have another hip replacement surgery on his left hip. Walter was there once again to help Charlie through this process by taking him to the VA hospital in Miami to have his left hip examined by his doctor.

The doctor's diagnosis confirmed that Charlie indeed had to have another hip surgery to replace his left hip. Walter was there to take care of him during his second recuperation from hip replacement surgery. He once again cooked for him, cleaned his house, did his laundry, shopped at the grocery store for him, got his medications and help bathe and bandage his wounds. He also assisted him with going to the bathroom until he was strong enough and well enough to get back on his feet.

A friend in need is a friend indeed! Charlie and Walter's

relationship was a prime example of that. Over time and over many years our families became great friends.

Our family affectionately began calling him Daddy Charlie! He became a father figure to my husband and another grandfather to our three children. Daddy Charlie moved to Climax, Michigan to be near one of his sisters. We often called and checked on him to see how he was doing and he did the same thing to us.

Love began to bloom and blossom with our relationship with our families. We began to know one another.

Where there once was hate for no good reason with Charlie, it grew into love. You can overcome evil by doing good.

Mr Charlie and Walter

Chapter 5

DUNKIN DONUTS COFFEE CREW

From left to right: John, Ron, Herb, Walter, Paul, and Jimmy

Walter is a member of the Dunkin Donuts Coffee Crew. The (DDCC) is a group of friends that meet early in the mornings Monday through Friday. They have a comradery together talking about various subjects, telling jokes, laughing and drinking their morning cup of coffee and having a good time together. They have been faithfully having these get-togethers for the past several years.

I guess you can call it a "Bromance" because they are all males.

Proverbs 18:24 says, *"A man that hath friends must shew himself friendly: And there is a friend that sticketh closer than a brother."*

They are from various social and economic backgrounds, employed, unemployed, self-employed, retired, semi-retired, business owners from all walks of society. They are republican, democrats and different shades of our society.

Each one has his own different view and opinion about any given topic. They may not all agree about some things; however, they know how to disagree without being disagreeable and still walk in love with one another.

What I like about this crew is that they are a friendly group and will invite anyone to join them at the counter or table. If they do not meet for coffee in the mornings, they will check on each other by calling, texting or a personal visit to each other's homes. Their friendship goes beyond the coffee counter or table. They are friends outside the donut shop. They are there for one another.

The Dunkin Donuts Coffee Crew has relocated and moved to another venue. They are now called "The McDonald's Coffee Crew." They still get together whenever they can.

PART II

THE MAN DEFINED

Chapter 6

OUR MARRIAGE UNION

Walter and I began dating in 1978. We dated for one and a half years before we got married on July 28, 1979 in Ocala, Florida. On our very first date, we went to the movies to see John Travolta in Saturday Night Fever. It was an awesome movie and we loved it.

I am truly blessed and honored to have been married to an incredible, God-fearing man for over forty-four years.

After our wedding, the very next day, we drove to West Palm Beach, Florida. This is where we began our lives together as husband and wife. Two people becoming one. Walter is the man of the house. He had goals right from the beginning and he shared those goals and dreams with me.

We knew we had to work hard and save our money together to get where we wanted to go. We also had to stay focused and to sacrifice. Early on in our marriage we discussed family planning and we decided not to have children right away.

Our first gift, Walter Cunningham Jr. was born on May 18, 1981. Our second gift, Cory Cunningham was born on December 11, 1985. Our third gift, Shayna Cunninham was born on September 19, 1988.

We decided not to look at our neighbors to see what they were doing, or try to keep up with them. We had a mission in mind and we stuck to it.

Chapter 7

THE EARLY YEARS

On my many visits to the home of Walter's parents,
I witnessed what real love was by experiencing it up close and personal with
the Cunningham family.

Mr. & Mrs. Cunningham were a very hard-working, loving couple with a very big family. They came from humble beginnings. They were the proud parents of eleven children, eight boys and three girls. My husband, Walter was their fifth child. They did not have a lot of money. They worked hard for what they got. They had lots of love and they freely shared it with everyone that they met—their immediate family, extended family, friends and even strangers.

Mr. Cunningham worked in the construction industry for many years to take care of his large family. Mrs. Cunningham was the homemaker who mostly stayed home to raise their children. However, sometimes she would do maid work cleaning homes to earn money.

Walter and his brothers did different types of jobs to earn money. They picked peanuts, tomatoes, peas, beans, corn, okra, and oranges. They also worked in the watermelon fields loading watermelons on a truck.

To help feed his family his father, Lester, and his grandfather, affectionately called "Daddy Mack," planted all types of vegetable gardens during the year including peas, beans, tomatoes, okra, corn, squash, cucumbers, carrots, mustard greens, collard greens, turnip greens, bell peppers, white potatoes, sweet potatoes, cabbage, lettuce, silver beets, and broccoli.

In addition to having gardens, they also raised biddies that grew up and became chickens and they also raised small pigs that grew into large hogs. Whenever the hogs became large enough, they invited their extended family, friends and neighbors to come over to their home and they would kill hogs for food to eat. They also killed the chickens to help feed their family.

Mr. & Mrs. Cunningham were very generous. They shared the various portions of the hog with their extended family, friends and neighbors.

Although they had a big family, they were not selfish. They selflessly and willingly shared what they had with others regularly.

On numerous occasions when I visited his parent's home, I noticed that they always had lots of friends which included white males and females. The friends also ate dinner with their family. Once I saw one of his father's white male friends sleeping on their living room floor.

Some of my husband's father's friends were his co-workers. They interacted and socialized at each other's homes. This was a wonderful and beautiful sight to behold and that is the way that it should be in our society. People should be loving on each other, enjoying one another's company and caring for one another regardless of their skin color.

Anyone who ever visited the Cunningham's family home in Ocala, Florida would never leave empty handed. Mr. & Mrs. Cunningham were always very kind and generous. They freely shared whatever they had with others.

I vividly recall on numerous occasions when my parents and other people visited their home, before they would leave, Mr. Cunningham would give them food such as uncooked meat, chicken, fish, from their deep freezer, or fresh vegetables or canned and preserved jarred vegetables.

Mrs. Cunningham was an excellent cook. She was masterful at cooking and preserving fresh fruits and vegetables by canning and putting them into glass mason jars. Canning means a method of preserving food from spoilage by storing it in containers that are hermetically sealed and then sterilized by heat.

Mr. Cunningham was also an excellent cook. He would cook breakfast, lunch and dinner and would invite other family members and friends to come to their home to eat.

I fondly recall many times overhearing my future father-in-law to be, calling different family members to invite them to come and eat.

There is a phrase that the "an apple does not fall far from the tree." This means in connection with children who show qualities or talents that are similar to those of their parents.

This is so true about my husband's parents and him. His parents, Lester and Evelyn Cunningham were a loving and devoted couple. They were personable and kind-hearted. No one was considered a stranger because they treated everyone that they met like members of their own family regardless of who they were and no matter if their skin tone was black or white.

Chapter 8

CAREER PATH

In March of 1979, Walter's uncle, James Yancy, invited him to come to Pratt & Whitney Aircraft to apply for a position. He told him to see a certain person when he got there.

Pratt Whitney was founded in 1925 and is a government company that built jet engines for the military. Walter took his advice and left Ocala and drove down to Palm Beach County, Florida. However, when Walter arrived at Pratt & Whitney, he did not see the person his uncle told him to see. He saw someone else who told him that they did not have any openings.

Subsequently, his uncle James followed up with him to see what happened. Walter told him that he saw someone else. His uncle reiterated and demanded that he go back to Pratt & Whitney to see the person that he told him to see about a job. Walter did as he was told. He saw the man he told him to see. In addition, he applied for a position and the rest is history. He was offered a position at Pratt & Whitney. He became a loyal and devoted employee who worked there for thirty-eight years.

Walter was a young man at the age of 24 years old when he began working at Pratt & Whitney. As I previously mentioned, he came from very humble beginnings and had the DNA and make-up of his father and his mother.

Chapter 9

CORPORATE SPOTLIGHT

Pratt & Whitney Rocketdyne West Palm Beach employee, Walter Cunningham, is featured in the second Diversity Spotlight article.

Employee Spotlight: Walter Cunningham

This is the second in a series of Diversity Spotlight articles that will be posted on FULL PWR.

Walter Cunningham began his career at Pratt & Whitney on March 26, 1979, as a parts runner on the Assembly floor for the JT11, Blackbird program. He was responsible for moving parts between the warehouse and assembly floor.

Cunningham worked diligently for six years before being assigned to the raw materials area to make parts. His conscientiousness and attention to detail was observed by leadership and was subsequently offered to opportunity to work in the Quality Department as an inspector. He became proficient in his new field through learning to read blueprints, perform dimensional inspections and successfully complete multiple on the job training opportunities. His broad-based knowledge has earned him respect within the Quality organization.

As a result of his dedication, expertise and work ethic, Cunningham was promoted to his current position: Lead, Receiving Inspection and Quality Review (QR) Crib.

"This position requires me to interface with Quality Engineers, Procurement and Production Control daily in order to ensure that parts produced meet the required quality standards," said Cunningham.

When asked to describe his career highlights, Cunningham said he considers his greatest achievements as being a mentor to, and developing good working relationships with co-workers regardless of their cultural background. He attributes this to his family background and upbringing, where he was raised with seven brothers and three sisters. Adding, I always remember where I came from and I take nothing for granted, and my goal is to treat others the way I want to be treated."

For Cunningham, diversity means working effectively with individuals of various cultural backgrounds and respecting their point of view. "I recognize that we all are capable of making meaningful contributions based on our respective culture."

Cunningham enjoys his job, and believes it's a great job that provided the opportunity for him to support not only his family but his community and his fellow co-workers and friends. He says "It's been great—no complaints—I'd do it all again."

Cunningham is known for greeting co-workers by saying, "thanks for coming in!" He stays in touch with former co-workers and continues to pattern his life after those he admires.

He has been married for 34 years to Audrey Cunningham. Their mantra is that they are willing to sacrifice for the destiny they have set for themselves and their two sons and one daughter.

Chapter 10

A MAN AMONG MEN

Please see the following things that my husband Walter has done and some things he is still doing throughout many, many years:

For fifteen years he hosted and financed the Cunningham Family Reunions in Ocala, Florida. He paid all the expense of purchasing the food needed for everyone.

They came from far and near to attend the family reunions. In addition, he reserved, booked and paid for a suite of rooms for family and friends to stay in at the Hilton Hotel.

He always said his motto is whenever anyone comes to our hometown, we always roll out the red carpet and give them first class and royal treatment. We make them feel welcome and give them our best. He wants everyone to be happy and have a good time!

He has surprised, treated and paid for breakfasts, lunches and dinners for recipients who were immediate & extended family members, friends, church family, acquaintances and strangers.

On numerous occasions, he has anonymously purchased breakfasts, lunches and dinners for people standing in line behind him at restaurants. He also has paid the toll for people coming behind us on the turnpike.

Many times when he went to the grocery store, sometimes while standing in line behind someone, he would overhear that a person in front of him did not have enough money to purchase their groceries. He would give them the extra money needed so that they could buy their groceries. The people were pleasantly surprised by his generosity. This is the kind of person he is. He gives from the heart and never ask for anything in return.

He has washed our neighbors cars when they did not ask him. Once we had a neighbor who was sick and out of work for a while. My husband gave his wife money so that she could buy food or pay some of their bills. He gave them money until he was able to go back to work. Years later, this same neighbor purchased a very large RV camper. My husband took down the fence in the back yard that separated our two properties so that the neighbor could park his RV camper in the backyard. He never charged him anything for parking it on our property.

Once, he booked and paid for a cruise for a couple that needed a vacation.

For many years, while commuting back and forth on the Florida turnpike to see our family, we sometimes would stop and assist other motorists whose cars had broken down due to a flat tire or car trouble on the side of the road. He has changed many flat tires.

We had friends that were having car trouble with their vehicles. Walter would give them the money, not loan it to them to get their cars repaired. He also has fixed cars himself and repaired family members, friends and acquaintances cars when they were broke down. He never charged them anything to fix them. When friends had their cars in the shop to be repaired, he loaned one of our cars to them until they could get their car fixed at no charge.

Numerous times my husband has cut our neighbors grass when they did not have a lawn mower or loaned our lawn mower to them so they could cut their grass. He also has given lawn mowers away to people.

For many years now, he has opened up bank accounts for children in order for them to have their own savings account. He direct deposited weekly out of his own personal payroll account into their savings accounts to help them. He also has helped young people who have gone off to college by purchasing the books that they needed for their classes.

My husband, Walter Cunningham Sr., is a phenomenal person. I am not saying this because he is my husband, I am saying it because this is the truth. He is a very loving kind, caring, compassionate, considerate and the most selfless person that I know.

He truly loves people and would literally give anyone the clothes off his body and the shoes off his feet and would do anything to help anybody.

He has a great BIG heart. He is a man who possesses enormous character traits. The fruit of the spirit runs through his veins. The Bible says the fruit of the spirit is love, joy, peace, patience, kindness, goodness, faithfulness, gentleness, and self-control. He loves to share his wisdom, knowledge and life experiences with others. He can carry on a conversation about any topic with anyone. I tell him that he has the gift of gab.

He especially like to share his knowledge with the young people. He has helped many young people in our community including our three children who are now adults and their friends. Many of our children's friends did not have a father in their household. They were being raised by their mother, so my husband was a father figure to them. For example, he would tell them to stay in school and get a good education. Education is key and necessary for success and knowledge is power.

After they get their high school diploma, they can go farther and go on to college. If they cannot go to college go to a trade school in their field of interest. If they are not interested in going to college, they should get a job and work hard to be the best employee that they can be.

He constantly tells young people to save their money. When our two sons were younger, he taught them how to wash and wax cars, how to mow the lawn, how to shampoo carpet and how to clean and wax floors.

He also taught our children's friends how to wash cars and cut grass. We taught our children to respect the elderly and to help them whenever they needed help. We emphasized to our children to help people and do not ask for anything in return which also meant do not ask for any money. To greet their elders by saying yes ma'am and no ma'am. Yes, sir and no sir.

He also taught them that money is a tool; do not spend it or blow it. I have witnessed first-hand what he does and has done for people over many, many years.

Every day of my husband's life, he looks for opportunities to be a blessing to everyone he meets. He constantly goes above and beyond the call of duty not only for his immediate and extended families, but also to friends, neighbors, acquaintances, enemies and even strangers.

Chapter 11

DRIVING MS. NETTIE

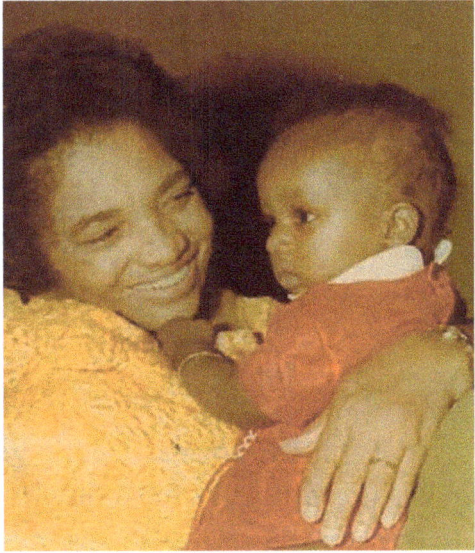

Ms. Nettie

While on his way to work, early one morning before daybreak, my husband saw an elderly woman walking in the middle of the street. He observed her walking in the street two more days after that and on the third day he slowed down his car to ask her why was she walking in the middle of the street.

The woman answered and told him that she was on her way to the bus stop to catch the city bus to go to work at her seamstress shop. She also said that she walked in the street because she did not want to be mugged or have anyone snatch her purse.

After hearing her story, Walter offered her a ride to her seamstress shop and she accepted. He did not want anything to happen to her, so he told her he would give her a ride to work every morning. He took her to her shop every morning before he went to his job at Pratt & Whitney. He did this continuously for approximately ten years or more. He would pick her up from her home and drive her to her shop.

My husband and the woman developed a friendship over the years. However, he did not know her name. When he talked about her, he called her "old lady." I told him that he should call her by her name and to find out what her name is. He asked her what her name was and she told him her name was Nettie. Out of respect, Walter began calling her Ms. Nettie. Lunette Dyke was her real name.

Taking Ms. Nettie to her shop became a family affair. On the days Walter could not take her, I would take her to her shop. If Walter and I had to go out of town during the week we would have one of our three children take Ms. Nettie to her shop.

We were teaching our children valuable life lessons, to have compassion for others and to help those that are less fortunate. Especially, help the elderly and those who are disabled. If someone wanted to offer them money, we taught them to say "No, thank you." Whatever you do, do it from your heart. God is the one who blesses us.

Our dear sweet friend, Ms. Nettie, passed away October, 1, 2016. We will always fondly remember her.

Chapter 12

LIFE SAVER

Several years ago, Walter helped save a young man's life who had been brutally assaulted and beaten in the head and robbed. The young man's name is Walter Stewart.

Early one morning around 2:00 a.m., Walter got out of bed and went outside in the front yard. He noticed someone staggering down the side walk. Walter started walking down the side walk towards the person staggering and as he got closer to him, he looked at his face and realized that he knew him. He lived in our neighborhood and was one of our former tenants.

The young man also named Walter, was trying to get inside an apartment next door to where we lived. He was very disoriented and thought that the apartment was his apartment. However, it was an apartment that he formerly lived in. Several months earlier, he had moved somewhere else. Walter told my husband that he wanted to go to sleep.

Walter knew from the serious injury to his head he should not go to sleep and told him he could not got to sleep. He kept talking to him and encouraging him to stay awake. He was bleeding very badly from his head. He called 911 right away to get help for him. The ambulance and the police came quickly.

Walter had a large gash in his head. He was rushed to the hospital. The doctors had to do immediate emergency surgery on him to save his life. They had to remove a portion of his skull to prevent swelling in his brain. We prayed for him and called to check on him at the hospital. Due to severity of his condition, he was placed in the intensive care unit for several days.

Thank God he survived! A few days later we visited him at the hospital. Walter was able to recognize us and knew who we were. It was a miracle because he was in his right mind and he had no brain damage. To God Be The Glory!

Walter remained at the hospital a while until he was well enough to get out of the hospital. After he was released from the hospital, he had to go to a rehabilitation facility. He later got well enough to be released. Walter's former teacher heard about what happened to him. She invited him to come live with her and her family. He agreed to move in with them. They took him up north and took care of him.

Walter Stewart never forgot that Walter helped save his life. He often calls to check on him and Walter calls to check on him as well.

Chapter 13

THE BLESSED VAN

Above is a photograph of the Blessed Van that my husband drove everywhere for over ten years. He drove it locally, out of town and on the turnpike. It was a total surprise when he received this special van back that Emory Griffin had painted for him.

I want you to take a little trip down memory lane with me when this occurred. As previously stated, it was ten plus years ago when my husband spoke to Emory Griffin, a family friend who was in the business of painting vehicles. The original color of the van was white and he wanted it repainted. Emory agreed to paint it. Walter did not tell Emory what color he wanted the van painted. He just left it up to him to decide on what color it should be.

The van was taken to Bradenton, Florida to be painted and it was several weeks later when he got it back. To Walter's surprise and amazement it was beautifully and uniquely painted the way it was with a picture of the Bible, the word Blessed, a Cross on the left side of it, a few books of the Bible written on both sides of it, praying hands, one white hand and one black hand together in the front of it and one white hand and one black hand in a hand shake on the back of it. Emory told Walter that he painted the van the way he saw him which is a testament to the true man that he is, a man of God.

Walter admitted that he was a little hesitant about driving the van around. He had to watch what he does and what he says when he was driving it. It is a moving billboard and it represents Jesus Christ! Don't get me wrong, Walter will admit that he is not perfect, He is a human being and there will always be times that he will be tested especially when you say that you are a Christian. People will observe him to see if he will make a mistake. Thank God he took care of this when he went to the cross for our sins.

When you are in the body you will make mistakes. When we make mistakes, we must repent quickly and ask God for forgiveness. When he forgives us, we should strive not to make the same mistake.

There were times when he was driving the van and someone did something that he did not like. He was tempted to say something to that person and he remembered that he was in the van. He could not say anything that was opposite of what the van represented about God and what was written on the outside of the van.

One day we were riding in the van coming back into town from Ocala, Florida when somebody was driving over into our lane. Walter had to quickly swerve to the right side of the road to avoid that person from hitting us. There was another driver behind the car that almost hit us. He passed by and said "God is Good!" We replied back to him that "God is Good!" Somebody was always watching him especially when he was driving around in that van.

We as Christians should always be mindful that Jesus is watching us every day of our lives and we must be good representatives for him. Being a Christian is being Christ-like. One day a man saw the van and noticed that there were only a few books of the bible written on the outside of the van. There are sixty-six books in the Bible. The man said sarcastically to Walter there are only is a few books written on the van. Where are the other books? He answered him and said that the other books were in him.

As the years began to roll by, we began to see the wear and tear on the van. The paint started fading, chipping and falling off. The door on the driver side no longer closed and he had to replaced it with another door. When the engine blew in the van, he bought another engine and had it installed.

Some of our family and friends began to continually tease and ridicule him about driving the van because of how it looked. They would tell him to get rid of that old thing and buy something else to drive. He did not let what people said deter him. He continued to drive the van where ever he went—to work, to church, locally, long distance, out of town and also on the turnpike. Some people told him that they saw him driving the van on the turnpike. He drove the van until 2022. He met a man in a parts store and the man told him that he needed a van. He told him that he had a van and he freely gave it to him. It was still in good working, running condition.

Chapter 14

COMMUNITY OUTREACH FOOD DISTRIBUTOR

My husband, Walter is a very personable human being who loves people and is passionate about helping anybody in any way that he can. I affectionately call him my social butterfly.

In the midst of the Covid-19 Pandemic, he was asked by his friend and former co-worker, Damon Ware, to help distribute food to people in the community.   He quickly took action and responded by doing just that. Once a week, rain or shine, still to this day he drives his pick-up truck to the distribution site and loads his truck up with food such as milk, dairy products, meats, bread, cakes, donuts, cookies, canned fruits, canned vegetables, fresh fruits, fresh vegetables, pastas, noodles, beans and peas. He would drive throughout the neighborhoods house by house. He would unload and deliver the food to anybody that wanted food.

Sometimes, I accompany him to the distribution sites where they also had people drive-through in their cars and pick up food. Food insecurity is real. Having a lack of food does not discriminate. People of all races—white, blacks, hispanics, and chinese come to the food distribution site looking for food on a regular basis.

There are people that are employed, underemployed and unemployed that need food to eat. A person can be working with a full-time job making full-time wages and still does not make enough money to buy enough food because of inflation. Everything is going up except their wages. The cost of rent is high, utility bills are high, gasoline is high, food is high, car insurance is high and homeowners insurance is high.

As I stated previously, food insecurity is real and it does not discriminate. I have seen people driving Mercedes Benzes, Lexus and Cadillacs, drive through the free food car line. We are blessed to be a blessing to others in any way that we can. When my husband and I drive around into various neighborhoods to distribute the food to the people they are pleasantly surprised and very happy to see the packaged and boxed food delivered to their door steps.

The smile on their many faces says a lot! Getting involved and making a difference is very important.

Nobody, and I truly mean nobody, men, women and children should ever be without food or go to bed hungry! We as Americans live in the greatest country in the world, the United States of America where food is plenteous and bountiful. Serving the needs of the people is what it's all about! We as people should never look down on anybody. It is by the grace of God on any given day at any time we could be in their shoes.

Chapter 15

MOTHER'S DAY
LUNCHEON SURPRISE!

My husband, Walter, is very thoughtful, kind and considerate and he is always full of surprises. Many years ago, he came up with this wonderful idea to treat our mothers to a luncheon for Mother's day. This luncheon did not just include his mother and my mother. He also invited his aunts, cousins and one of his sisters to join them at the luncheon. He told me about it and I loved it! It gives us great joy making people happy!

They all lived in Ocala, Florida. We planned a trip for them to go out of town for the luncheon. So, we selected a restaurant in Gainesville, Florida for them to go to have lunch. In addition, he rented a limousine to go to each one of their homes to pick them up. They had no idea that a limousine was coming to get them. One family member saw the limousine pull up at another family member's house and thought it had something to do with an undertaker and a funeral.

The photos below are extra special. Giving that special loved one their flowers while they are alive. In other words, show love to a person quickly while they are alive so they can see it and feel it! Don't wait until they are dead and gone. The first photo is my dearly beloved mother-in-law, Allean Cunningham. The second photo is my dearly beloved mother, Elizabeth Thomas Bryant, in the lime green dress. She has since passed. She died on March 1, 2011, one day after her 70th birthday. Her birthday was February 28, 1941.

Also gone but never forgotten are Walter's Aunt Eloise Summer, dressed in white, Aunt Burnise Cunningham, dressed in pink, Cousin Mary Tindal, dressed in blue and his Cousin Beatrice Webster, dressed in the printed shirt and black pants. His sister, Olivia Watson, is dressed in black.

Not in the photo was Walter's aunt, Algene Hopkins and his cousin, Nolan Webster, Jr.

Allean Cunningham,
Walter's Mother

Elizabeth Bryant,
Audrey's Mother

Audrey's Mother
heading to
the limousine

Limo driver, Elouise Summers, Bernice Cunningham,
Mary Tindal, Olivia Watson (still living), Beatrice Webster

Chapter 16

WALTER'S DOLL

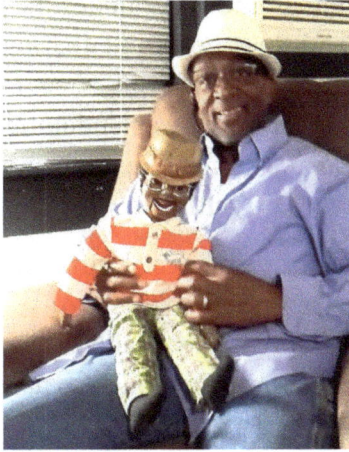

Yes, you did read this correctly. Walter has a doll that was designed and created to look just like him. It was a total surprise to him when his friend Bill presented him with a Christmas present in a large box. He had no clue what was inside of the box. When he opened it up, to his surprise, it was a ventriloquist doll that resembled him.

Walter met Bill several years ago at his special spot—Dunkin Donuts. A brotherly bond and friendship emerged when other men joined the early morning get-togethers for coffee and conversations and they became known as the Dunkin Donuts Coffee Crew.

You can see in the above photograph, little Walter and I do mean the doll. He has a small round face with brown eyes and he has glasses on his face and a mustache just like his twin. In addition, he has an afro and wears a trademark hat like Walter likes to wear. He also has his mouth open. This is another great description of Walter because he loves to talk. I have told him on many occasions that he has the gift of "gab".

My husband is never at a loss for words. He can strike up a conversation with anybody and go on and on talking. He involves himself into some very interesting topics and not so interesting topics and does not mind sharing his thoughts and opinions on any given subject. This is who he is and what he does best. Sometimes, if we have an appointment and have to go somewhere, I have to tell him to keep his conversation brief. If he does not, we would be late getting to where we need to go.

Mini Walter is an extra special gift made from Love. Bill unfortunately passed away a few years ago. When Walter looks at the mini-Walter doll he remembers and cherishes fond memories of his friend, Bill, who thought enough to have a doll made after him.

Bill, seating in the meddle, creator of the Walter doll and his family

Chapter 17

BROTHER/NEIGHBOR JOHN

John Burns was a neighbor that Walter initially met at Dunkin Donuts weekdays, Mondays through Fridays. He was one of the members of the Dunkin Donuts Coffee Crew. They quickly became close friends and he later became one of our tenants. John confided in Walter that he was diabetic. After learning of John's illness, Walter regularly stopped by John's house or called him on the telephone to check on him to see how he was doing.

John was a single man who did not have a wife or any children. He did not have any family that lived in the local area. They all lived up north. Their brotherly friendship lasted for many years.

One day Walter went to John's house. He knocked on the front door and there was no answer. He also called John's cellphone and it rang and rang and there was no answer. Later that day, Walter found out that John's boss went to his house because he didn't show up for work. That was not like him. He knocked on the door and he didn't answer the door. So, he used John's house key that he had given him. When he went inside his apartment, he found him dead.

Walter contacted John's sister by telephone to let her know that her brother had passed. His family were unable to come to Florida to take care of his final arrangements. So, John's sister asked Walter to mail John personal papers to her. In addition, she asked him to thoroughly clean out his apartment. She also told him that he could keep all of the contents of his apartment. John's sister told Walter that John was very fond of him and that he always talked about him to their family.

Walter reminded John's sister that John had a nice-looking pick-up truck and she should come and get it. She told him that he could keep the pick-up truck. John would want him to have it. I helped look through John's personal paperwork to find the papers that his sister needed and in addition, I helped clean the apartment.

You never know who you are going to meet on life's journey. It is very important to be kind to everyone that you meet. Matthew 22:33-39. *"Thou shalt love the Lord thy God with all thy heart, and with all thy soul, and with all thy mind. This is the first and great commandment. And the second is like unto it, Thou shalt love thy neighbor as thyself."*

PART III

TESTIMONIALS OF LOVE

Chapter 18

LLOYD HAMILTON, CURRENT CO-WORKER AND FRIEND

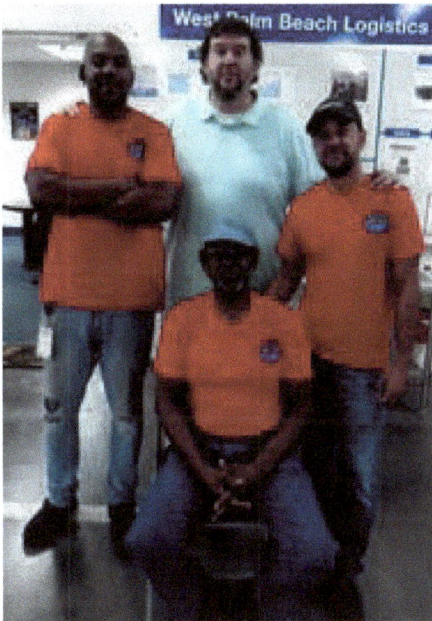

Walter and his Aerojet Co-workers

Standing: LLoyd Hammilton, Eric Longshore and Mike Gonzalez

Seated: Walter Cunningham

I have been knowing Walter Cunningham for six years and he has never changed. He also goes out of his way to help others. He never hesitates to demonstrate kindness and Christian-like lifestyle. Walter is a true example of hard work and dedication. He is a true friend indeed when you need him. We work together and we exercise together. I just want to say that God has truly blessed me with a great and amazing friend.

Chapter 19

MIKE GONZALEZ, CURRENT CO-WORKER AND FRIEND

I began a new job in February 2020 and had the pleasure of meeting a man named Walter Cunningham. As a newcomer, meeting new people can be nerve-wracking, but Walter made me feel comfortable and brought laughter to the workplace.

Over time, I noticed the kind gestures he would do, like bringing in donuts or breakfast, which made a positive impact. However, I soon realized it wasn't just the items he was bringing, but something more valuable—love and care for others. Walter's belief in staying true to himself and not changing has stuck with me. He truly embodies the importance of kindness and compassion towards others.

I am grateful to God for blessing me with a job that not only provides for my family but also allows me to help others that cross my path. God has blessed me not only with this job but also with a kind and giving colleague. Walter exemplifies the love that

Christ has called us to share with our neighbors. It is inspiring to see Walter's actions matching his words and witnessing firsthand the impact of doing for others what we would want them to do for us. Jesus teaches us, *"Wherever your treasure is, there the desires of your heart will also be.* (Matthew 6:21 NLT)

Mr. Cunningham's way of living by these principles is inspiring not just to me but to others as well. Our daily conversations at work uplift me and remind me why we, as Christians, are here. He has not only spoken about the love that Christ has placed in his heart but also lives it. This has enabled those around him to see the true love of Christ.

"So follow the steps of the good, and stay on the paths of the righteous. (Proverbs 2:20 NLT). One thing I love about Mr. Cunningham is he shares his life experiences so that we don't fall short in life but exceed in it.

Thank you, Walter Cunningham, for being who God has created you to be and stepping out, pouring out with love to those around you and living out the word's that are written in Philippians 4:4-9.

Chapter 20

WILLIAM "BILL" CLINTON, FRIEND AND FORMER CO-WORKER

William Clinton, Walter, Darth Vader, Audrey, Storm Trooper, Beverly Morrison

William "Bill" Clinton began working at Pratt & Whitney Aircraft in 1972 and met Walter Cunningham in late 1979 or early 80's. He remembered on one occasion when he and Walter were on the dock at work, Walter saw someone shorter than he was and he gave the guy a $1.00 bill. Walter told him that if he met anybody shorter than he was that he would give that person a $1.00. Walter is 5 feet 7 inches tall in height. He is short is stature but stands very tall as a Man.

Bill said that Walter had a way about him and he was always humorous and generous. He recalled many times Walter would bring boiled eggs to work to share with his co-workers. Everyone at work came together and began looking forward to him bringing in the boiled eggs. They began talking with one another and socializing together. They began to have a camaraderie. Walter also began bringing to work dozens of donuts and would freely distribute them to his coworkers.

Everyone looked forward to seeing him at work. If he did not come to work everyone would ask where he was and would be concerned. They wanted to know if he was okay. Bill also said that he and Walter had similar backgrounds. Both of them came from large families and they came from humble beginnings and had to work hard when they were younger by doing various jobs. Some jobs were hard manual labor, they helped their families financially to make ends meet.

Being around Walter and associating with him one cannot help but want to be like him. It is a saying "association bring on assimilation." This is how he felt about Walter. Walter helped him to change for the better.

No one was a stranger to Walter. He would go up to a person and introduce himself and began conversing and getting to know that person. Bill said that Walter would light up a room. He always had a genuine character and loved people. He also said that he knew Walter was a righteous man and knew he loved God. He showed and demonstrated it by how he loved and treated people.

Bill said when he had his retirement party, he was completely surprised to see so many people were in attendance. It was because Walter had invited them to come to the party.

Many times he witnessed Walter pay other people's tab for breakfasts and lunches.

Bill also vividly remembered when his mother was not feeling well. Walter made a copper bracelet for his mother and gave it to her. Before that time Walter had not met his mother. There is a saying that a copper bracelet helps older people in pain with arthritis.

He considered himself to be truly blessed for having met Walter Cunningham when he did. His character rubbed off on him. Even though he was always a giver, Walter taught him how to be a better giver and how to give more.

William "Bill" Clinton considered Walter Cunningham to be the Dr. Martin Luther King Jr. of Pratt & Whitney because he brought people of all races together.

Chapter 21

ELDER JAMES MARTIN, FRIEND AND FORMER CO-WORKER

The best I can say about Walter Cunningham is I know him. According to the Bible, A man is blessed if he has one friend in a lifetime. Walter is everything that you look for in a friend.

One thing I can say about Walter is he knows how to treat white people. They are always doing something for him or giving him something. He knows how to say thank you and sincerely mean it. At Pratt & Whitney Aircraft, he had more white friends than he had black friends. I also like the relationship he has with his wife. She is a great woman in her own right. I love and respect both of them. There are so many good things to say about them and this book would not hold it all.

Chapter 22

DEBBIE JONES, FRIEND AND FORMER CO-WORKER AT BARBIE'S RESTAURANT

Debbie Jones and Walter Cunningham

If you had to pick one word to describe Walter, it would be Generous. He would give you the shirt off his back. He is kind, caring and funny but don't underestimate him. He has a very good business sense and he isn't easily fooled.

He makes friends in all walks of life. If you mention the name Walter Cunningham in a room full of people, everyone in that room would have nothing but kind words to describe him. He has been my friend for over thirty years and hopefully we have at least thirty more years to go.

Love you, Walter

Chapter 23

MY BEST FRIEND,

by Kenny Harbin

In January 1983 at the age of 22, I began a new job at Pratt & Whitney Aircraft (PWA) in South Florida. That same week, I joined a local gym, "Muscle Junction." This particular gym had been recommended to me because it was "Hard Core," with lots of serious lifters and competitive bodybuilders. As a guy who took his workouts seriously, I wanted a Hard-Core gym.

One of the appealing attributes of this particular gym was a sense of community, the feeling that everybody knew everybody, even if you weren't necessarily best friends. And because I was in the gym six days a week, it was only a matter of weeks before I knew almost everybody by their first name. Muscle Junction was a great fit for me. I was making friends, and I was really happy there.

Late in 1983, probably around November, I was at work one day, and I noticed a guy wearing a Muscle Junction t-shirt, I was surprised that he was not at all familiar to me. He looked fit and in good shape, but. I had never once seen him in the gym, so I assumed the t-shirt must have been perhaps given to him. Out of curiosity, I stopped and asked him about the t-shirt, and he informed me that he was an active workout enthusiast at Muscle Junction…my gym! So, I introduced myself as Kenny, and he introduced himself as Walter…but I noticed that those around him referred to him as "Ham" (it turns out that his last name is Cunningham, and he often goes by the nickname ("Ham"). He was warm and affable, outgoing and friendly, and just seemed as genuine and good-natured as a human being could be. I found myself instantly liking him.

Still, in the back of my mind, I wondered how in the world… in 11 months…is it possible that I've never seen this guy in the gym, not even once! Was he really a member of my gym?

That same day, after I left work, I headed to the gym for my daily afternoon workout, and as I walked through the front entrance, the first person I saw was…you guessed it…Walter Cunningham, the same fellow I had met earlier that day for the first time. What a surprise! He saw me and waved me over, and invited me to join in his workout. So we trained together that day, and…even though neither of us knew it at that moment… we began what would turn into the most amazing and treasured lifelong friendship that any person could ever hope for!

Over the next 5-6 months, the friendship slowly grew, and what began as occasionally meeting up at the gym to work out together, gradually grew in becoming permanent workout partners who trained together daily. And for the record, if you've ever been a serious weight lifter, then you already know that working out with a partner is far preferable to working out alone. Partner workouts tend to be more intense, more extreme, and far more productive.

At work, we began having lunch together every day. During

this same period, Walter introduced me to his family...his wife Audrey, and his young son Walter Jr. His family was just like him...kind, warm and friendly. Walter Jr referred to me as "Uncle Kenny."

In May of 1984, I competed as a heavyweight in the Mr. West Palm Beach Bodybuilding contest, and although I won no trophies, I was so motivated and inspired by the experience that I committed to spending the next twelve months investing all my time and energy into preparation for the 1985 Mr. West Palm Beach contest. My goal was nothing less than a first-place trophy, and needless to say, I would need to know that my training partner shared my deep sense of commitment. When I spoke to Walt about my intentions, he was fully on board and ready to invest just as much effort as me. There was never any doubt in my mind that he wanted me to win just as much as I wanted to win! This was going to be a team effort, and I knew he'd be with me every step of the way.

Over the next twelve months, our friendship grew even closer, and we became something akin to "blood brothers." In addition to the grueling daily workouts, we would often ride to and from work together, and were now having both breakfast and lunch together at work. We also started a Saturday morning tradition that continues to this day, breakfast at the IHOP.

In May of 1985, the Mr. West Palm Beach contest finally arrived, and it was time to find out if all the hard work and dedication had paid off. Walter picked me up that morning and we drove to the auditorium for the pre-judging. The pre-judging takes place in the morning and afternoon, while the actual show itself and trophy presentations take place in the evening. I was both kind of excited and kind of nervous. Walt was definitely excited and much less nervous. He was very reassuring to me, and his demeanor was one of confidence. He helped me oil up and get ready, then waited patiently while the endless rounds of posing dragged on. When the pre-judging was finally over, it was late afternoon, and the actual show was only two hours away. We grabbed a quick bite to eat, then returned for the moment of truth!

When all the individual posing routines were over, it was time for the trophy presentation. As the top three heavyweights were called to the stage, my pulse raced as I heard my name! Third place was called out, followed by second place…and neither name was mine! I was the First Place Winner! An attractive blond walked on stage and presented me an enormous trophy, and the rest is history! It was one of the greatest thrills of my life!

Kenny Harbin, bodybuilder

After the show ended, we were backstage getting dressed, and gathering our things, and then as we walked to the car, Walt proudly carried the large trophy. He was just as elated as I was! And in that moment, I suddenly realized the amazing depth and magnitude of our friendship! We weren't just "workout buddies," we were best friends. We were a team. He had invested a full year of hard work and commitment, just as I had.

Now, I suppose if our friendship had just been built around the gym and bodybuilding and winning a trophy, then it would have begun to erode after the contest. But instead, the bond flourished and grew stronger. Later that year, Audrey gave birth to their second son Cory, and I had a new nephew! Walt was not only my best friend, but his family was my family.

In May of 1986, he and I decided to do a Mother's Day Road Trip. We would leave home early and drive to Ocala to have lunch with his Mom, then stop in Palm Bay on the way back and have early dinner with my mom. Simple, right? Well, maybe not. I had recently purchased a used VW Scirocco. It ran great, got really good gas mileage, and was a few years old…what could go wrong?

So early Sunday morning we jumped in my Scirocco, headed north to Ocala, and had lunch with Walter's Mom. Other than some rainy weather, everything went well, and the drive was easy. Mrs. Cunningham is quite a character, loaded with personality and energy, and very easy to talk to (it's easy to see where Walt gets his personality). She was extremely pleased that we had made the trip. I really enjoyed meeting her, and was honored to share Mother's Day with Walter and his Mom.

After lunch and some good conversation, It was time to leave, and head back south toward Palm Bay. Having just filled our bellies, we deliberately took the "scenic route," hoping that we would have an appetite by the time we arrived. We got to my parents' house by late afternoon, and they were ready and waiting for our arrival. Mom and Dad had already heard many "Walter stories," so they couldn't wait to meet him. We sat and enjoyed Mother's Day dinner with them, while Walt talked about his family and told several of his entertaining anecdotes.

After dinner we said our goodbyes. There was still plenty of daylight remaining when we left for the final ninety minutes of our road-trip. Everything had gone perfectly. We got to meet each other's Moms, enjoy really good food, and also see our own Mom for Mother's Day. What a day!

About forty-five minutes after we left Palm Bay, disaster struck. We were heading south on I-95, when suddenly the car just simply shut down. We weren't out of gas, the engine was not overheated…it just died. We coasted to a stop near Fort Pierce, still about forty-five minutes from home.

There were no cell phones in 1986; therefore, we desperately needed to get to a payphone so I could call my Dad. Fortunately… or so we thought…there was a building just off the highway that appeared to be similar to a junior high school, or maybe a high school. We assumed there would definitely be a payphone somewhere on the premises, so we didn't think twice about crossing the interstate, scaling the fence and exploring the property. We could even see a bunch of guys off in the distance playing basketball on an outdoor court.

As we made our way across the large, open field, we noticed a moving golf cart off to our right, coming straight toward us. Hopefully, this guy could point us in the direction of the payphone…or maybe even give us a ride!

About twenty-five feet away from us, the gold cart stopped, the guy quickly got out...overweight, wearing sunglasses and a uniform...and pointed a shotgun straight at us, while shouting "Put your hands up or I'll blow your f*cking heads off!". And as if this wasn't bad enough, he had this look on his face that suggested he WANTED TO SHOOT US!

We were simultaneously shocked...terrified...confused...all while trying not to pee in our pants.

He then had the decency to ask..."Just what in the hell are you guys doing here?" We were happy to reply.

We explained that our car had broken down, and we needed to find a payphone. He listened as if he couldn't believe what he was hearing, then finally said..."Just when I thought I'd seen everything, apparently you two sh*t-heads are completely unaware that you have illegally entered into the Fort Pierce Correctional Facility. Congrats, you're the first two assholes in history to BREAK INTO a prison!"

Seriously...it wasn't a school. It was a prison. And we climbed a fence to GET IN. Let that sink in...

Well, at this point, all we really wanted was to leave, so we politely asked if he'd let us out, and he said..."You're going out the exact same way you came in"... and he marched us all the way back to the fence, and stood watch while we climbed back out. Honestly, we were just happy to be alive.

We hitched a ride to a payphone, called my Dad who came to our rescue. We made it home safe and sound. The last thing I said to Walt that night was...We can NEVER tell anyone about this! This will be our secret, and we'll take it to the grave. No one can ever find out!" And he agreed. This story would never be told. Never.

The next morning I got to work and walked in the cafeteria, and heard several loud voices yelling across the room…"Hey Kenny, broken into any prisons lately?"

Apparently, Walt's ability to keep a lifelong secret lasted for about eight hours. That's Walter!

Looking back, I guess those were the crazy days of our youth when we had big muscles and unlimited energy, and it seemed like we were always on-the-go. But no matter how much you might want to stay young forever, time passes, life brings changes, and next thing you're middle-aged…or older. And although our paths has diverged at times our friendship has always remained solid and unwavering.

In 1988, Walt and Audrey had a daughter, Shayna, their third child, my niece! She is absolutely gorgeous!

In 1995, Audrey threw a surprise 40th Birthday Party for Walt in Ocala. Naturally, I attended. When he walked in and everybody shouted "SURPRISE", he said casually…"I knew something was up when I saw Kenny's truck outside."

In 2005, Audrey threw a surprise 50th Birthday Party for Walt, and I was the DJ! It was a blast!

And then last year, 2022, I finally married the love of my life—Nabiyah—and only invited a small handful of friends to the ceremony. Walt and Audrey esteemed me with their presence. After 40-something years as a happily married couple, they wanted nothing more than to see me experience that same happiness. It meant the world to me that they attended.

As I mentioned earlier, life often brings changes, sometimes very unexpectedly…which is exactly what happened a few months ago in November 2022 when I got the surprise of my life. Through the miracle of DNA, I found out I had not only a thirty-six-year-old daughter—Britney—but also three grandchildren!

At the age of sixty-two, this was probably the most unlikely news I could have imagined! I was ecstatic!

When I told Walter and Audrey about Britney, they were simply overjoyed...and dying to meet her! I took her over to their home on a Sunday afternoon. We intended to stay about thirty minutes...and ended up being there for hours! They were thrilled to meet her and hear her life story. They just could not get enough of her. For me, it was overwhelming seeing their outpouring of love for my daughter, and for me too. Walter's face was one of pure happiness in the knowledge that my lineage would indeed carry on.

And as of now, that's forty fantastic years of friendship in a nutshell, with many more years to come. In retrospect, Walter's presence in my life has not only brought fun, laughter, and adventure, but it has also benefited me in countless ways and made me a better person. In actuality, he has been much more than just a "friend, he has indeed been a blessing from God.

Audrey Cunningham, Nabiyah Harbin, Kenny Harbin,
Walter Cunningham

Chapter 24

IN LOVING MEMORY OF MY DEAR FRIEND, MR. JOHN DALE KELLER

By Walter Cunningham

Walter Cunningham and John Keller

In 1979, when I started working at Pratt & Whitney Aircraft in Jupiter, Florida, I walked around inside the building where I worked observing everybody in my department. Mr. John Keller stood out displaying a lifestyle of a Christian.

He was a soft-spoken gentleman and showed great love for people. He had a character about himself that was different from the rest of the people that I worked with and as the years went by, I got to know that Mr. John Keller was a great man. Over time, the more Mr. John and I hung together the more we fell in love with each other and became great lifelong friends.

I found out that he loved God very much! Mr. John was very gifted and multi-talented. He was blessed with an amazing singing voice. I vividly recall hearing him sing for the first time. I was an instant fan.

He was also very talented with building things out of wood. He made kitchen cabinets, tables, and beds. He regularly made kitchen cabinets for his home, family members, friends, his church and for other people. He put his heart into everything that he made and everything that he made came out beautiful.

Mr. John and his family lived in a beautiful home in Lake Park, Florida. I visited with him at his home often and we got to know each other very well. We later began carpooling to and from work. Shortly thereafter, our families got acquainted with one another. My wife and three children got to meet his beautiful wife, Mrs. Charlotte and their children: John David, their youngest son; Becky, their youngest daughter and her children Shana and Josh. Later on, we met their older children, Jerry and Beverly who lived elsewhere. Mr. John and Mrs. Charlotte loved and adored their children and grandchildren and talked about them all the time.

Our families hit it off and we began co-mingling together. We visited their home and they visited our home. We often broke bread together having breakfasts, lunches and dinners.

Mrs. Charlotte was a very sweet and kind woman. She was also multi-talented. She was an excellent cook and everything that she made was very delicious. She was also an excellent seamstress and made beautiful dresses and clothing. Mrs. Charlotte made two beautiful dresses for our daughter when she was a little girl.

In addition, she also was an excellent housekeeper and always kept their home always clean and organized. Whenever we stopped by their home for a quick visit, everything was always in place.

As I reminisce of decades of friendship with Mr and Mrs. Keller and their family, we will always cherish and fondly remember that we were blessed to have had them as great friends. We were involved in many wonderful milestones in our families lives.

Mr. & Mrs. Keller invited my wife and I to a play that John David was in when he was at Cardinal Newman High School. The play was The Pirates of Penzance of which he played a starring role. We were pleasantly surprised and blown away when we heard John David sing for the very first time. Before then, we did not know he could sing. He has an amazing beautiful melodious voice like his father. He could sing very loudly and can hit very high notes and hold it for a very long time.

They also invited us to their church. At that time, they were members of the original Christ Fellowship Church in Palm Beach Gardens, Florida where Tom Mullins was the Pastor. One day, we took them up on their offer and visited the church. We received warm and friendly greetings from everyone. We thoroughly enjoyed the service.

Years ago, when our children were younger, sometime our family would stop by the Keller's home after church to visit them.

I would go into their house and say hi and would leave my wife and children sitting in the car.

They would be having dinner and at times they did not have enough food for everybody so, I would sit at the table and eat dinner with them. They would ask, "Where is Audrey and the children?" I told them that they were outside in the car. They would laugh and think that I was joking. They realized it wasn't a joke; that it was the truth.

They said, "Why didn't you bring them in?" I said to them, "Well, I didn't think you had enough food and it was no sense of me bringing them all in." We all just laughed and had lots of fun.

After thirty plus years, Mr. John retired from Pratt & Whitney. They later sold their home in Lake Park and relocated to Ormond Beach, Florida where their daughter, Beverly Powell and her family lived. Their son-in-law, Gary Powell, was the Pastor of Oasis Fellowship Church. Their new home was beautiful and it had a pond near it. The church was approximately one and a half miles from their new home.

We sometimes would drive through Ormond Beach on our way to Ocala and would stop by and visit Mr. and Mrs. Keller. A few times we stayed overnight with them.

Although the Kellers had moved to Ormond Beach, they continued to travel back and forth to West Palm Beach to see family and friends. They would stop by our home for a visit. A few times they stayed overnight with us.

In May of 2007, our daughter, Shayna was graduating from Palm Beach Gardens High School. We invited Mr. & Mrs. Keller to her graduation ceremony. Without hesitation, Mr. & Mrs. Keller drove all the way from their home in Ormond Beach to West

Palm Beach, Florida in support of her for this special occasion. To be in attendance at her graduation at the Convention Center to cheer for her, meant the world to us. Mr. John thought enough of us to come to our daughter's graduation even though he was ill and had not been feeling well. They made it their business to be at her graduation.

Mr. and Mrs. Keller are both gone now. We will never forget them for they will always hold a special place in our hearts as dear friends.

Audrey & Walter Cunningham, Charlotte & John Keller

Chapter 25

IN LOVING MEMORY OF HAROLD BRITTAIN

Provided by Steven W. Brittain, son, on behalf of Harold Brittain, a longtime friend and former co-worker of Walter Cunningham

Walter Cunningham, met my dad in the late 1970's, around 1979. They immediately became the best of friends. My dad always looked past the color of a person. He tried to look for the good in people. He grew up poor in Oklahoma with native Indians as his neighbors. He gave everyone a fair chance as far as friends go, regardless of race, age and gender, but think what bonded dad and Walter was their love for family. Dad loved my mom and us kids unconditionally. I think dad saw that in Walter.

He wasn't a player or a fool for other women. He and dad were pretty dang handsome in those days. But that respect and love for family was their strongest bond. They also both had a strong faith in the Lord and the Bible.

Dad had a lot of friends, but I have to say, Walter was one of the very best of my dad's friends. Dad brought Walter to the house when I was probably about 15 or 16 years old. I'll never forget his politeness, his beautiful laugh and smile and always joking.

And boy was he in shape too. He had some big muscles too. So me, my dad and Walter (we call him Ham) became very close friends and we are still friends today. A unique bond was formed that day with my entire family, Like I said, dad had a lot of work friends, but very rarely did he invite them home to meet his family. So we knew Walter was very special. I know dad trusted Walter too. They worked together for over 28 years in the same department and never once did I ever hear my dad speak a bad word about Ham ever. Ham would come visit us and still does today, he loved my mom, sister and Grandma as well. He would make her laugh until her stomach would hurt, teasing her about pulling chicken off the bone for the dogs, even after the dogs died, she would still do it...lol.

Divine intervention – My mom passed away in March of 2021. We had kept dads ashes around since 2018, so we could bury our parents together where they wanted back in Oklahoma Redlands Cemetery. Only close family and friends knew we were having this service.

Saturday, May 15th 2021 on the way to the service with my parent ashes in my lap, I got a phone call from Walter. He called and said, "Hi Steve Brittain, what are you doing today?"

Low and behold I told him, "I am on my way to bury my parents."

We both could not believe it. So after thinking about it Ham said he did not recall calling me; it was like a "butt dial" or something. We both to this day believe it was my dad's way of connecting us one more time for his sake and for the long friendly relationship they had over the years.

I feel it is very important to share this because my dad was like that. Dad would always call people at the right time when they needed to hear from him. I needed that call from Walter that day and it helped me so much. I think my dad was looking down on me and that was his way of helping me cope by hearing from his best friend Walter.

Lastly, I have been to several weddings, anniversaries and company outings, with Walter. I want to tell you the most important thing he ever told me. This is still clear in my mind as I am writing this. "When you get married and have a family, you put all those foolish things away." I really believe this faith and love for his wife Audrey and his sons Walter Jr., Cory and daughter Shayna is what bonded my dad with Walter.

I think and know a lot of people feel the same way. I have an admiration for him, to see how hard he's worked. Even though he was very successful, his love and generosity was extended to anyone who needed it. What a beautiful milestone of 44 years together with the person you love most. So many people envy your love, but I find it very beautiful.

Chapter 26

MRS. ELIZABETH HOOE

Former friend and neighbor, Roberta Jurney daughter sharing on behalf of her mother

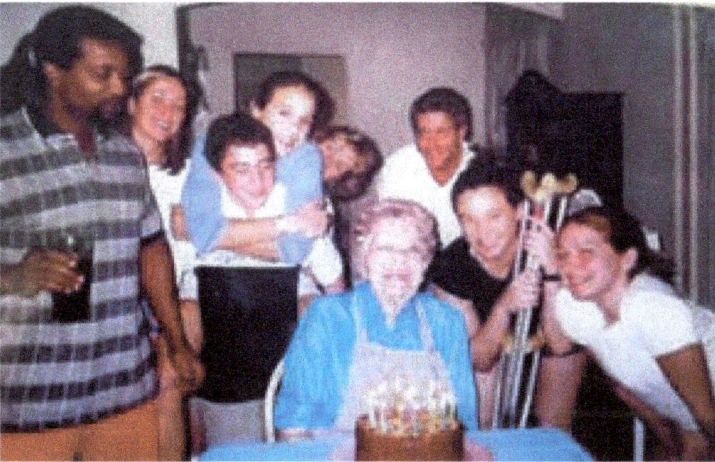

Seated, Mrs. Elizabeth Hooe, surrounded by family and friends

Walter befriended Mrs. Elizabeth Hooe in the 90s. Mrs. Hooe was a sweet, elderly, neighbor who lived four doors down the street from our home in Lake Park, Florida. Mrs. Hooe was a widow with three daughters. Walter was introduced to Mrs. Hooe by Charlie Waychoff who lived next door to her.

After Walter's introduction to Mrs. Hooe, they became very good friends. He began visiting her on a regular basis to check on her to see if she needed help with anything. He also did various odd jobs for her around her home. She affectionately began calling him the Prince of Silver Beach Road.

Shortly thereafter, Walter brought our two young sons to visit Mrs. Hooe. He later assigned them the tasks to help her. He had them do chores for her, sweeping and mopping her floors. He was teaching them a very valuable life lesson at a young age. He taught them to respect their elders and to help them whenever they needed help. In addition, he told them never to accept any money when they do something to help people. He also told them that God will bless them for what they do for others.

Roberta Jurney, one of Mrs. Hooe's daughters, shared that her mother loved Walter, his visits and his friendship. Just sitting and talking with him meant the world to her. In addition, she said that she will always be so grateful to him.

Roberta also recalled when her mother became ill and had to be hospitalized and placed into the Intensive Care Unit. While she was in the hospital, the family was informed by the hospital staff that she could only be visited by her immediate family members.

One day, Walter went to visit his friend, Mrs. Hooe at the hospital. Upon his arrival at the hospital, he told the hospital staff who he was there to see. The staff told him that she could only see her immediate family members. Walter told them that he was Mrs. Hooe's son.

Sadly, Mrs. Hooe passed away in 2001. Later that year, Mrs. Hooe's daughters asked Walter and I if we wanted to purchase their mother's home. We agreed to do so. In 2002, we purchased the home and fast forward, twenty-one years later, Walter and I are living in the home that Mr. Hooe built for his family in 1925. Our family is the second family to live in it. The home is full of love and fond memories of the loving friendship and relationship between Mrs. Hooe and Walter and both of our families. We will always cherish the relationship.

FINAL CHAPTER

Walter Cunningham's life is a prime example of a pupil obeying his Heavenly Father by living the greatest commandment: LOVE.

The testimonials shared in this book confirm the fact that Walter Cunningham is truly A Man Among Men.